LinkedIn: 30 Highly Effective Strategies for Attracting Recruiters and Employers to your LinkedIn Profile

Land the Job of Your Dreams!

A.J. Robbins

Author's Note

Thank you for purchasing my guide, LinkedIn: 30 Highly Effective Strategies for Attracting Recruiters and Employers to your LinkedIn Profile. Before discussing the strategies, I would first like to discuss a little about LinkedIn. LinkedIn is the world's largest professional network consisting of over 300 million people worldwide. It is a social network that allows professionals from all over the world to form a "connection". Connections should only be formed if the person with which you are requesting to connect with is known. The larger the connection list that you build up, the better for you and your future job opportunities.

Recruiters and Employers both say that LinkedIn is their number one resources for recruiting and hiring new employees. This is why it is imperative you follow this instruction manual on searching for keywords, creating a complete LinkedIn Profile, and managing current information updates to your LinkedIn Profile.

This book offers information on adjusting your LinkedIn URL, linking your Social Media and LinkedIn Profile, and creating a Headline that grabs the attention of search engines and potential employers. There is also information on contacting old classmates and school chums, connecting with professional groups, and even using volunteer activities to your advantage on the LinkedIn Profile.

There are also various sections on the do's and don'ts of social media and LinkedIn. There are some common mistakes people make that virtually eliminate them from a potential career in a promising field, all by foolishness. This guide will help you pinpoint those career bombs.

You need this book to utilize every tool available to you through your LinkedIn Profile. Using the methods and information included in this book will change the way you are listed on search engines and employee recruitment files, allowing you to be considered for the job of your dreams!

I would advise taking **massive action** after reading each of the strategies, this will give you a greater chance of success in optimizing your LinkedIn profile.

Table of Contents

Profile Hacks

Chapter 1: Keywords are the Foundation for LinkedIn Visibility

Fortune 500 companies recruit directly from LinkedIn, and the primary element in reaching their attention is the use of keywords in your profile. To access these relevant words, look at the profiles of people with the job position you desire. What are the words that show up time after time? Those are the keywords that you should include in your profile, to attract the attention of recruiters and human resource personnel.

Once you have discovered the keywords, place them in your job descriptions, your profile title, and in the Summary description of your profile. Another pivotal placement is in the Groups section of your LinkedIn profile. Do not include these terms if you do not have experience in these areas. Falsification of your qualifications can result in termination.

What if you don't know what the most useful terms should be? Google the job title you desire, and search those resumes on LinkedIn. Google will also suggest similar terms for you to use. An example would be: Internet marketer, when googling it suggests content marketing, online marketing, informative content marketing, return on investment (ROI), for just a few terms. Adding these terms to your LinkedIn profile will ensure appropriate recruiter offers.

Chapter 2: Be a Visible Presence on LinkedIn

It does you no good to just put a simple resume on LinkedIn. LinkedIn is built for networking and search engines. You must have an extensive resume that lists your accomplishments, service work, industry groups, professional connections, and most important of all, keywords.

Flesh out your resume by using the Summary section, and make sure your keyword is listed at least two times. Take advantage of the Jobs section to list your keywords in your accomplished and experience job functions. Have an updated photo in the appropriate attire you wear for you professional position. Many recruiters bypass resumes just because there is not a photo attached

Get more visibility with links, pdf files, and videos that are attached to your profile. Did you get an award for an outstanding performance? Attach it to your LinkedIn profile. Do you have copies of your last exceptional performance review? Make a pdf and attach it to your profile. Do you have letters of reference or recommendations? Place them in the file, also. Any clickable link or pdf makes you more noticeable to a potential employer.

Chapter 3: Your Profile Summary is Your Job Application

Make it strong and aggressive. This is the time to boast and shine, not be modest and humble. You want your Profile Summary to reflect your skills and expertise. Your enthusiasm for your job should be obvious to the Recruiter.

Don't forget your keywords because these are the basis for the candidate job search. Weave your keywords into your Profile Summary in a natural way. Discuss accomplishments in the keyword categories. List your skills and include the keywords.

Use shorter sentences to highlight strengths. Shorter sentences attract more readers than long, dense copy. It is better to bullet point information that to list 3 lines of sentencing. People like to read in lists and microbursts of information.

Utilize breaks in information by incorporating boxes and lines for a visual impact. Adding a border before and after a section, using the bold font to highlight your name, italicizing job skills or performance reviews all allow the eye to travel in comfort. Be careful to use no more than three visual differences on your job profile, or the effect will be a cluttered, disorganized profile. The eye can only process 3 or 4 changes on a page without having focus problems.

Chapter 4: Completely Fill In All Details of Your Employment History

Too often a potential employee leaves out relevant details on their resume. Past positions reflect your maturing job skills. Employers want to know if you have served in the Armed Forces, no matter how long ago this happened. Veterans have proven leadership skills, are able to take orders, and prove that they can carry through an objective.

Utilize this area to list your accomplishments. Make a bulleted list of tasks and achievements with statistics and measurable information. An example is: reduced accounts receivable balances by 28% in the first month of collections. Your potential employer wants to know what you do and how well you perform.

Highlight your best features in the Job Descriptions category. Balanced $18 million in cash receivables daily, for example. Reconciled accounts and applied payments. Customer service through verification of deposits and payment entries. All of the above statements use keywords in their information. In this case the Google keywords were verification, reconciled, balanced and customer service. Remember keywords are the foundation for most employee job searches. Be sure to Google the keywords that are utilized in your job market.

Chapter 5: Completely Fill Out the Entire Profile

Leave nothing blank. You don't know what the qualifications are for every job in your situation. The fact that your hobby is quilting shows a potential employer that you are both creative and exacting, as quilting requires exact measurements to ensure the quilt can be sewn together and creativity to be able to mix patterns, colors, and textures.

Some employers spend as much time in the Education, Groups, Volunteer Activities and Languages as they do in the active Job skills sections. Your education verifies that you have the ability to stick to a task, even when repetitious. Your group activity enhances your marketability skills through attesting your desire to be current with technology. The volunteer activities exhibit your ability to work with others from various backgrounds and cultures. Your foreign language abilities are always a plus in today's global marketplace. Update those sections with relevant information about your current activities; this might just be the information the employer is seeking. Be sure to make the Profile keyword dense.

Chapter 6: Show Evidence of Your Skills by Linking Samples

This is where you incorporate current marketing trends with evidence of proven accomplishments. Link samples of your work through attached pdf files or YouTube videos. Potential employers and recruiters want verification that you utilize current technologies, as well as look at the type of work you produce.

Make a LinkedIn portfolio of your work. LinkedIn will accept Word, Excel, PowerPoint, pdf files, and photos attached to your LinkedIn Profile. Have an example of each of these to demonstrate your skill in utilizing these products. Employers want to know you have basic computer skills, and these products are now the foundations of business communications.

Your portfolio should be an example of both your creativity and your expertise in the field. If your keywords are Business Management, have a document file of a schedule you have created, a spreadsheet that you regularly update, an example of your communication style with an interoffice memo, an example of a completed project you managed, and an example of a method or procedure you have developed. The latter is a great opportunity for a PowerPoint presentation.

Chapter 7: Show Your Skills and References

If you have an endorsement or special skill, give an example through a pdf file upload. You can list up to 50 skills in LinkedIn. Take the time to comb resumes and job applications of the dream job for which you are applying, and then apply those skills to your personal LinkedIn Profile. List all the skills for which you have experience and aptitude.

Utilize keyword searches to determine which skills are searched for most frequently. These are the skills you want to place in your LinkedIn Profile. If you have a letter of reference or a recommendation, place a pdf in your LinkedIn Profile. This alleviates the recruiter's need for verifying that statement and looks good when they peruse your file

Chapter 8: Make Your Profile and Activities Keyword Friendly

I cannot emphasize enough the importance of keywords in your job search. If the recruiters can't find your LinkedIn Profile, they will not hire you. Make your Profile visible to them by using keywords in every area of your Profile.

Do not be too specific in your job title unless it is the only job title you will accept. Instead, list three titles for which you are qualified, separated by bars.

Pick the top three keywords for your job, and then incorporate them into your Profile in various areas. Change your LinkedIn URL to reflect who you are and what you do. Instead of having John1234567 at LinkedIn.com as your URL, change your URL to LinkedIn.com/in/JohnSmithengineeringandITpro.
This tells a recruiter instantly what you can accomplish.

Search engines and recruiters both use keywords to skim through the resumes of persons that want the job but don't have the qualifications. Display your qualifications by using keywords in the Title, Job Descriptions, Summary and even Volunteer Activities. Customize your URL to list job functions with your name. A distinctive URL will attract the attention of potential employers and recruiters.

Chapter 9: Display a Current Professional Photo!

Include a recent photograph in your LinkedIn Profile. Make this professional shot in appropriate workplace attire. One of the underlying questions in a recruiter's mind is whether there will be a problem with you following workplace rules, policies, and regulations. The best way to exemplify compliance is in your personal dress code. Always opt for conservative versus casual in a professional photograph

.

In the Volunteer Activities section you can include a more relaxed photo. Always make it a photo with a pleasant smile. You want to give the impression you can get along with everybody and that you are companionable to your co-workers.

One of the most common reasons for workplace termination is the violation of company policy. This covers a lot of territory, but you want your portrait to exemplify and obedient and professional personality with high standards and morals. No one wants to hire a creepy, disheveled high school bum that wears outdated clothing of a questionable nature.

Chapter 10: Give Evidence of Your Credibility

When updating your LinkedIn Profile, prove your skills by attaching pdf files with examples of your work, projects, and pictures. Include company awards, prizes, letters of recommendation or commendation, bonus acknowledgements, or any evidence you have of a job well done.

Create a portfolio of useful information like projects completed with pictures and annotations, any awards or prizes you may have earned, any accomplishments in your private life, any membership cards or miniatures of your diplomas or transcripts, clues to who you are and what you have chosen for priorities in your life.

You can add a section in the portfolio for your volunteer activities, those things for which you have a passion. This is where you can shine in displaying your most important strengths. You want your potential employer to see you as a knight in shining armor that can solve the problems of his kingdom.

Make your best assets known in your portfolio. If you are top of the class in a learning environment, include a pdf of the certificate. If you have perfect attendance, every employer is interested in this specific job trait. Make a copy of your pdf or your employee attendance record for the file.

Chapter 11: Social Proof: Linked (In)

Recruiters often say the first thing they do is compare the resume in hand to the LinkedIn Profile online. Next they go to the Social Media and check for a Facebook page. They compare jobs and remarks, blog posts and comments. If you have listed different jobs or information on either place it will be immediately obvious.

If you have detrimental personal information posted on your Social Media, now is the time to get rid of it. Your Tweets, Comments, Blogs and Facebook Posts are all linked in the Internet and will be read by your potential employer or recruiter. This is not the place for eccentric posts regarding politics or social causes.

Do not post fraternity party photos or any embarrassing photos in bathing suits. Do not list your hobbies as "mummy collector" or "sex God or Goddess."

It may not be fair, but Social Media posts are the reflection of who you are and what you represent. Do not jeopardize a potential career by posting silly or profane remarks. Clean jokes are fine, but dirty jokes are not. Do not post anything you would not want attributed to you if it were read in front of a large crowd, because, essentially that is what you are doing. You are broadcasting your personal business and attention to millions of people every day.

Chapter 12: Customize Your LinkedIn Profile's Headline for Searchability

Change your headline to include those important keywords for optimum searchability. Instead of just listing in your headline John Smith, IT Consultant, list a headline like this:

John Smith, CIO and IT Specialist/Creating Global Technical Support Response Teams

Make your headline sing your accomplishments and attract the attention of recruiters and potential employers. Focus on your strengths and areas of expertise, your demonstrable skills, and your optimum assets and qualifications for your employer.

Search Google keywords to determine what needs to be in your headline to attract the potential employers in need of your specific skills. Use those keywords in prime categories so that the search engines will pull your name from the pool of job seekers. Keywords can make the difference between a findable resume and Profile and one lost in the shuffle. There are 3 unemployed people for every job opening. Use all the tools that LinkedIn gives you to make your LinkedIn Profile notable to the recruiting professional.

Chapter 13: Connecting with LinkedIn's Education Tool

When completing your LinkedIn Profile, be sure to supply all your educational connections in the form. List every school you have attended, even if you did not graduate or complete the course. Next, select the tab "Interests" from the drop-down menu at the top of the page. Run down the page until you see "Education," and press this tab. Select "See Your School," this will tell you how many alumni are on LinkedIn, and what groups are available for membership.

Use this connection. Look for friends and acquaintances on the list. Contact them and update them on your job search and your needs. Ask what you can do for them. Make suggestions of ways you can mutually help one another. Do not ask for a favor if you do not have a favor to offer first to them. Do not be a user or taker; you should begin a reciprocal relationship.

Chapter 14: Customize Your LinkedIn Profile's URL

The standard URL for LinkedIn users looks like this:

LinkedIn.com/in/JohnSmith1234567

But you want to be hip and noticed, so you change your URL to this:

LinkedIn.com/in/JohnthebestITprogrammerSmith

This is how you do it:

Go to your LinkedIn Home page,

1. Click "Profile"
2. Click "edit profile"
3. Find the box with your URL, and then click the edit pen.
4. Then find the area that says your public profile URL, hit the blue edit pen,
5. Then edit the link with 5-30 letters and no spaces,
6. It must be original to you, so MarySmith won't be available, MarySmith/accountingpro/ probably would.
7. Save

Network, Network, Network!

Chapter 15: Have a Large Network

Networking is no longer about quantity; instead it's all about quality. This is reverse from the information that was formally promoted, "get all you can to connect."

What you need is 20-25 dependable people that know you well. These are the people that will be hoping to promote you in your job search. Maintain contact with these people 3 or 4 times a year, updating them on your current availability. These should be the people with whom you are socializing.

The next group of people will number 100 or so. These are friends and acquaintances that will give you a positive recommendation. You will send them Social Media blurbs or links to your accomplishments.

The last group of people is the "rest of the world." This might be your Christmas card list. All you want to do is keep your name fresh in their mind.

If you want a real connection with someone, do something to help him or her. Even the richest man in the world has personal and professional needs. Find out what they care about and then find a way to help them in this area. Maybe they are interested in pet rescue. Send them a well-made video of a local pet shelter or a donation in their name.

Be a generous person and offer your help at every opportunity. Be interesting and lively. Make the person want to know more about you.

Look around your circle for the persons that go above and beyond in every endeavor. Copy their actions so that you develop the same habits. You want to project leadership and power, not weakness and banality.

Chapter 16: Make New Connections

Do not keep yourself hidden from new connections. Move outside of your comfort zone and connect with people that share your hobbies or volunteer activities. Take a risk and a new responsibility. If you are unemployed at this time, this is the opportunity to update your skills by taking a college course or a vocational course.

Use rejection as a motivation for your job search instead of a detriment. Ask the contact why you were rejected and listen carefully to the response. The real answer may be between the lines of the reply. Instead of saying your photo was unprofessional and they fear you would be too casual in your adherence to company policies, the recruiter might say, "You have a very eccentric style of dressing." Try to discern what the real objection is to your employment.

Making new connections could be contacting the rejecting recruiter to offer to meet a need of theirs. Stretch outside of yourself and befriend people you usually avoid.

Chapter 17: Include Your Alumni in Your Connections

Now that you have found your old friends and buddies add them to your network. Send them family newsletters, business links, and anything that will keep you in touch. Seek them out for social applications and connections, like the local youth soccer team. Join them for coffee and snacks at Starbucks, visit their church and synagogues, whatever place that you can talk and renew your acquaintance.

These old and familiar connections can be a new source of employment referrals, as we shall discuss in the next strategy. Treat them with the respect that you and they deserve at this period of their life. Don't call them vulgar names or remind them of their teenage body odor. Connect with them in a positive way with lots of kindness and forgiveness.

Chapter 18: Employers that Seek Alums from Your School

Under the "where they work" tab, look to see if clusters of your alumni are employed with one employer. Go to that employer website to look for open job positions. Under the "show more" tab you will see cities, locations and more data about alumni from your college or professional school. Also look at the skills listed to see if you need to add categories to your LinkedIn Profile.

When approaching the potential employer, drop names of fellow students that are in their employ. Say something like, "I noticed that Steve Smith is enjoying a career in your Internet Marketing Division, it is his connection to me through University X that prompted me to inquire about any openings in the Social Media Marketing Division."

If you drop someone's name, inform him or her you have used the connection. Don't blindside them by arranging for a contact from Human Resources to confirm your school connection or attendance. Give them ample notice to prepare a statement for Human Resources.

Chapter 19: Using Education data for relocation

When you are checking the Education and Alumni information, make note of the groups of former students by locations. It is advantageous to accumulate a list of target locations for persons with your same school major and same job keywords. Calling these classmates is a good way to renew your connection and ask about their current location and job. They can give you the inside and personal information about the city and the employer, things you won't get from a Chamber of Commerce website or a company profile, even on LinkedIn. As an example, my grandfarther was once placed in a nursing home because of a stroke. The reviews of the nursing home talked about the wonderful, personal care given by the nurses. No one discussed the food palatability. He lost 38 pounds because of the disgusting food. There were no references anywhere regarding the food, but it would have been mentioned immediately by a current resident.

Chapter 20: Participate in Industry Groups

It is just as important to join professional groups, as it is to have experience. Employers desire to know that you are engaged in the current and progressive changes in your field, and proactively seeking experience and knowledge. Nothing will date your resume more than a long list of experience but no updated contacts.

If you are not a social person, join the professional groups that meet once a month, or less. Join the fraternities or sororities that have thousands of members so your absence at meetings won't be noticeable.

If you join a group online, be sure to participate. Recruiters log in to these groups to see who is knowledgeable and experienced in the field for which they are inquiring. Just being there, or "lurking," is insufficient for an aggressive job search. Participate and show your experience through constant contact with other members.

Check the resumes of people you admire in your field to see where they are gathering. Go there and be a presence that is known for sincerity and knowledge. Once or twice a week make a post that demonstrates your particular expertise. Don't comment on every thread, but do comment on a consistent basis.

Chapter 21: Utilize Social Message Boards to Your Advantage

Don't just hang out on social message boards, be an active participant in a site that is in your field of expertise. Open new threads of conversation, offer a solution to a problem, empathize with other employees about job issues, but not about employers. Do not ever criticize a previous or potential employer online. Every word you write online is recorded, catalogued, and cross-referenced.

When you engage other message board members you may be opening the door for your employment offer. Recruiters and human resource managers often hang out in professional message boards to seek the appropriate person to offer a position in the firm. They are looking for the best and the brightest, so showcase your knowledge of the industry by contributing regularly to professional message boards.

Use every outlet available to make contacts that you can then connect to your LinkedIn page. Put your LinkedIn URL at the bottom of your signature so it is imprinted with every remark you make. Use message boards as one more place to gather names and information, while leaving your tag for a connection point.

Chapter 22: Search for Current and Past Employees of the Employer for Whom You Wish to Work

Most recruiters give more merit to a resume from that has a personal reference of an employee than to job fair and recruitment resumes. For the aggressive job searcher, this means you need to connect with current and past employees of your dream job. This is where those online and industry connections through groups are utilized.

When conversing online, it is common to mention where you work and what you do. Connecting through mutual jobs functions, industry groups, and social functions will enhance your pool of potential employers. You don't know when someone is looking for a bright, new employee that can provide the solution for a common industry problem.

An example would be the Internet marketer, who has listed they are well versed in SEO. When discussing SEO in the group, mention the tactics that are used to verify a company is versatile and making a valid presence in the Google, Yahoo, and Bing rankings. Your visible knowledge of industry standards will make you conspicuous in a room of lurkers and petty chatters.

Another way to connect with present employees of your dream job is to go to the LinkedIn Company Profile for that organization. There you will have a list of key personnel of the organization. Check to see if you know somebody, maybe you went to high school with him or her? Search the Company Profile for job opportunities, groups that you can join, and points of action that you can insert your presence. If this is a company that supports St. Jude, for example, by sponsoring a 5k run each year, volunteer to be on the support team for the 5k run. Go to the meetings and make connections. Work hard for St. Jude. Someone from the group will remember you when a job opening appears as a hard worker that is unselfish and caring for others.

Chapter 23: Be an Active Participant in LinkedIn Groups

LinkedIn groups will be the first place that recruiters and potential employers will search for your name and activity level. Search on LinkedIn for professional groups that use the keywords for your profession. Recruiters use these forums to post job openings and search for potential employment candidates. Often they lurk in potential problem areas for the field to see who might exhibit the expertise for a useful solution.

Bring attention to yourself by posting well-researched questions that are problematic for persons in the field. Offer suggestions for solutions. Don't use this time to banter or chat, instead use this opportunity in groups to demonstrate your extensive knowledge of the field or issue at question.

Instead of empathizing with a well-known struggle, offer an inexpensive fix or suggestion to resolve the issue. An example could be that churches constructed before a certain time are grandfathered in and exempt from the handicapped accessibility issue. It is a known fact that churches are greying and more people need assistive devices. While it might not be affordable to install a $10,000 elevator in an older building so the members can go upstairs, it is affordable to install a $500 chair lift that will slide up the stairs to the second floor. This would be an affordable solution for those using a cane or a walker to access the second floor.

Chapter 24: Keep Updated Contact Information

If you want recruiters to contact you, they need to know your address, phone number, and website. Give them this information in your LinkedIn Profile so they know where you are located. Don't forget to exhibit your current email address also.

It doesn't hurt to have a Google Plus profile, as this is a searchable item for recruiters. Get a Gmail address and become a presence on Google. Remember your professional keywords and use them in all your blogs and web addresses. Keep all web information current so that recruiters will not be confused as to where you are and how to find you.

Having multiple contact points that are conflicting will frustrate the job recruiter, so audit your information on Social Media to ensure it is all the same. Make all your residences the same, all your email addresses into one, and your entire phone numbers alike.

Chapter 25: Using LinkedIn Connections Reminders

LinkedIn has a connections tab that lists all of your current connections from your email accounts and your online connections within LinkedIn. If you look at your connections tab, it will inform you of all your friends and their workplace anniversaries.

This gives you an opportunity to show mutual interest in their career plans while also renewing the acquaintance and friendship in a subtle manner. The connects tab has relationships listed in four categories.

Level 1 Connections are those people you have a personal relationship with through email.

Level 2 Connections are those people that know your friends in email and connect with them.

Group Connections are those people in your LinkedIn groups.

Level 3 Connections are those people in a similar field but are not part of your circle.

By utilizing all your Connections opportunities, you can expand your network and potential employers.

Using LinkedIn to Find a Job

Chapter 26: Stealth Updates for Your Profile

If you have decided that now is the time to begin searching for a new job, do not advertise it on LinkedIn unless you are no longer employed. Your employer will be reading updates on LinkedIn just like you do and most employers will fire someone for looking for another job because of the risk of corporate espionage.

Be stealthy in updating your LinkedIn Profile. Slowly update keywords and titles, not all at once. That is a red flag to your employer that you are seeking a job change. Make a habit of updating your Profile monthly by adding a skill, or contributing to a group discussion, or updating your keywords to reflect your growing responsibilities.

Make your employer look good by listing new opportunities that you have modified on the company's behalf. For example, if you designed the widget that offers the RSS feed say so, it makes your company look good for having one and you look good for designing it.

Chapter 27: Company Pages

Company pages display the vital statistics for a company and website. The company page should include the company name, logo, address, phone number, web address, email and sometimes even a map to the location. There should always be a link to the company website and a call to action. Frequently asked questions should be displayed.

An ideal Company Page will list a summary of services and objectives, current job openings, links to social media, videos, employee blogs and relationships, reviews from clients and customers, a great first image that captures attention, current updates and media information, a button to promote subscriptions or a call to action, and current events.

Chapter 28: Make Use of the Job Board on LinkedIn

LinkedIn has a very user-friendly job board for persons actively seeking employment opportunities. By going to the Jobs tab, LinkedIn walks you through a way to create a professional profile for job hunting. Don't limit yourself to a specific professional title as many employers change the title to reflect the required tasks. Internet Marketing Manager could be listed as SEO Manager, Social Media Manager, etc.

Make sure your headline has keywords for your desired job position. If you are unemployed, use the last title you used while you were employed. Do not list volunteer positions as current employers; this will skew the results of a search from a recruiter. You should only list paid positions on your LinkedIn Profile as employment. If you list a volunteer position, your potential employer will be confused as to why you are applying in a field for which you are not qualified.

Chapter 29: LinkedIn Update Feed

Make sure your update feed is displaying valuable information. Access your LinkedIn Profile and look under "all updates," then further down the panel to "your updates." Notice what is included and what is missing. Update those connections that are gaps in your information. Look for places where nothing is posted, update to round out your Profile.

This is where the importance of daily postings on blogs and groups becomes an asset. Through these postings your Profile is updated with your current activities. For a recruiter, this is a prime source of employment knowledge. Keeping up with your Update Feed is another maintenance activity, like Googling your name to see what links are provided.

Chapter 30: Group Jobs Tab in LinkedIn

The group jobs tabs have two functions, to show the jobs availability for LinkedIn jobs, and to show job postings for sources outside of LinkedIn. The tab marked "Jobs" is for the LinkedIn jobs. This feed is governed by the group manager who sets the automatic feed when he/she sets up the page. The tab marked "Jobs Discussions" is for jobs that are available outside of LinkedIn. These postings automatically expire after 14 days, whether or not they have been updated by the posting party to inform if the hiring is closed.

A Final Note

Thank you for downloading my book, LinkedIn: 30 Highly Effective Strategies for Attracting Recruiters and Employers to your LinkedIn Profile. By accessing and implementing these strategies I hope that you have already landed your dream job. In case you have yet to receive that magic offer, thoroughly engage each of these activities to ensure you have a keyword optimized LinkedIn Profile:

1. Update all your contact information and photograph,

2. Examine your Social Media broadcasts to ensure you give a professional demeanor in every circumstance,

3. Utilize and engage all of your network contacts to inform them of your current job search,

4. Update your LinkedIn Profile, heading and URL to attract recruiters and potential employers.

Effective involvement in all of the above strategies and the rest of the information included in this book will assure you the attention of employment recruiters.

Preview of Resume Writing 2016

Although LinkedIn to a large extent has replaced traditional CVs/Resumes, they are still a fundamental tool required to get you the job. They **should not** be ignored.

Resume Writing 2016 is a complete guide to crafting the perfect resume. It's available on the Amazon Store, go and check it here: http://amzn.to/1OLrjHb (Paperback, Kindle and Audiobook available!). For a limited time, it is available for $2.99 (usually $9.99) – what's more, if you purchase the paperback, get the Kindle book for only 0.99c!

Finally, if you enjoyed this book, I would really a review: http://bit.ly/reviewforme

Wishing you all the best,

A.J. Robbins.